baby sprinkle & co.
Find us at Amazon.com/Author/BabySprinkle

Copyright ©Baby Sprinkle & Co.™
All Rights Reserved.

Guests

NAME & RELATIONSHIP TO THE PARENTS

_____

_____

MESSAGE OR ADVICE FOR THE PARENTS

_____

_____

_____

WISHES FOR BABY

_____

_____

_____

Guests

NAME & RELATIONSHIP TO THE PARENTS

_____

_____

MESSAGE OR ADVICE FOR THE PARENTS

_____

_____

_____

_____

WISHES FOR BABY

_____

_____

_____

Guests

NAME & RELATIONSHIP TO THE PARENTS

_____

_____

MESSAGE OR ADVICE FOR THE PARENTS

_____

_____

_____

_____

WISHES FOR BABY

_____

_____

_____

Guests

NAME & RELATIONSHIP TO THE PARENTS

_____

_____

MESSAGE OR ADVICE FOR THE PARENTS

_____

_____

_____

_____

WISHES FOR BABY

_____

_____

_____

Guests

NAME & RELATIONSHIP TO THE PARENTS

_____

_____

MESSAGE OR ADVICE FOR THE PARENTS

_____

_____

_____

_____

WISHES FOR BABY

_____

_____

_____

Guests

NAME & RELATIONSHIP TO THE PARENTS

_____

_____

MESSAGE OR ADVICE FOR THE PARENTS

_____

_____

_____

_____

WISHES FOR BABY

_____

_____

_____

Guests

NAME & RELATIONSHIP TO THE PARENTS

_____

_____

MESSAGE OR ADVICE FOR THE PARENTS

_____

_____

_____

_____

WISHES FOR BABY

_____

_____

_____

Guests

NAME & RELATIONSHIP TO THE PARENTS

_____

_____

MESSAGE OR ADVICE FOR THE PARENTS

_____

_____

_____

WISHES FOR BABY

_____

_____

_____

Guests

NAME & RELATIONSHIP TO THE PARENTS

_____

_____

MESSAGE OR ADVICE FOR THE PARENTS

_____

_____

_____

WISHES FOR BABY

_____

_____

_____

Guests

NAME & RELATIONSHIP TO THE PARENTS

_____

_____

MESSAGE OR ADVICE FOR THE PARENTS

_____

_____

_____

_____

WISHES FOR BABY

_____

_____

_____

Guests

NAME & RELATIONSHIP TO THE PARENTS

_____

_____

MESSAGE OR ADVICE FOR THE PARENTS

_____

_____

_____

WISHES FOR BABY

_____

_____

_____

Guests

NAME & RELATIONSHIP TO THE PARENTS

_____

_____

MESSAGE OR ADVICE FOR THE PARENTS

_____

_____

_____

_____

WISHES FOR BABY

_____

_____

_____

_____

Guests

NAME & RELATIONSHIP TO THE PARENTS

_____

_____

MESSAGE OR ADVICE FOR THE PARENTS

_____

_____

_____

WISHES FOR BABY

_____

_____

_____

Guests

NAME & RELATIONSHIP TO THE PARENTS

_____

_____

MESSAGE OR ADVICE FOR THE PARENTS

_____

_____

_____

_____

WISHES FOR BABY

_____

_____

_____

Guests

NAME & RELATIONSHIP TO THE PARENTS

_____

_____

MESSAGE OR ADVICE FOR THE PARENTS

_____

_____

_____

_____

WISHES FOR BABY

_____

_____

_____

Guests

NAME & RELATIONSHIP TO THE PARENTS

_____

_____

MESSAGE OR ADVICE FOR THE PARENTS

_____

_____

_____

WISHES FOR BABY

_____

_____

_____

Guests

NAME & RELATIONSHIP TO THE PARENTS

_____

_____

MESSAGE OR ADVICE FOR THE PARENTS

_____

_____

_____

_____

WISHES FOR BABY

_____

_____

_____

Guests

NAME & RELATIONSHIP TO THE PARENTS

_____

_____

MESSAGE OR ADVICE FOR THE PARENTS

_____

_____

_____

_____

WISHES FOR BABY

_____

_____

_____

_____

Guests

NAME & RELATIONSHIP TO THE PARENTS

_____

_____

MESSAGE OR ADVICE FOR THE PARENTS

_____

_____

_____

_____

WISHES FOR BABY

_____

_____

_____

Guests

NAME & RELATIONSHIP TO THE PARENTS

_____

_____

MESSAGE OR ADVICE FOR THE PARENTS

_____

_____

_____

_____

WISHES FOR BABY

_____

_____

_____

_____

Guests

NAME & RELATIONSHIP TO THE PARENTS

_____

_____

MESSAGE OR ADVICE FOR THE PARENTS

_____

_____

_____

WISHES FOR BABY

_____

_____

_____

Guests

NAME & RELATIONSHIP TO THE PARENTS

_____

_____

MESSAGE OR ADVICE FOR THE PARENTS

_____

_____

_____

WISHES FOR BABY

_____

_____

_____

Guests

NAME & RELATIONSHIP TO THE PARENTS

_____

_____

MESSAGE OR ADVICE FOR THE PARENTS

_____

_____

_____

_____

WISHES FOR BABY

_____

_____

_____

Guests

NAME & RELATIONSHIP TO THE PARENTS

_____

_____

MESSAGE OR ADVICE FOR THE PARENTS

_____

_____

_____

_____

WISHES FOR BABY

_____

_____

_____

_____

Guests

NAME & RELATIONSHIP TO THE PARENTS

_____

_____

MESSAGE OR ADVICE FOR THE PARENTS

_____

_____

_____

_____

WISHES FOR BABY

_____

_____

_____

Guests

NAME & RELATIONSHIP TO THE PARENTS

_____

_____

MESSAGE OR ADVICE FOR THE PARENTS

_____

_____

_____

_____

WISHES FOR BABY

_____

_____

_____

_____

Guests

NAME & RELATIONSHIP TO THE PARENTS

_____

_____

MESSAGE OR ADVICE FOR THE PARENTS

_____

_____

_____

_____

WISHES FOR BABY

_____

_____

_____

Guests

NAME & RELATIONSHIP TO THE PARENTS

_____

_____

MESSAGE OR ADVICE FOR THE PARENTS

_____

_____

_____

WISHES FOR BABY

_____

_____

_____

Guests

NAME & RELATIONSHIP TO THE PARENTS

_____

_____

MESSAGE OR ADVICE FOR THE PARENTS

_____

_____

_____

_____

WISHES FOR BABY

_____

_____

_____

Guests

NAME & RELATIONSHIP TO THE PARENTS

_____

_____

MESSAGE OR ADVICE FOR THE PARENTS

_____

_____

_____

_____

WISHES FOR BABY

_____

_____

_____

Guests

NAME & RELATIONSHIP TO THE PARENTS

_____

_____

MESSAGE OR ADVICE FOR THE PARENTS

_____

_____

_____

WISHES FOR BABY

_____

_____

_____

Guests

NAME & RELATIONSHIP TO THE PARENTS

_____

_____

MESSAGE OR ADVICE FOR THE PARENTS

_____

_____

_____

_____

WISHES FOR BABY

_____

_____

_____

Guests

NAME & RELATIONSHIP TO THE PARENTS

_____

_____

MESSAGE OR ADVICE FOR THE PARENTS

_____

_____

_____

WISHES FOR BABY

_____

_____

_____

Guests

NAME & RELATIONSHIP TO THE PARENTS

_____

_____

MESSAGE OR ADVICE FOR THE PARENTS

_____

_____

_____

_____

WISHES FOR BABY

_____

_____

_____

Guests

NAME & RELATIONSHIP TO THE PARENTS

_____

_____

MESSAGE OR ADVICE FOR THE PARENTS

_____

_____

_____

_____

WISHES FOR BABY

_____

_____

_____

Guests

NAME & RELATIONSHIP TO THE PARENTS

MESSAGE OR ADVICE FOR THE PARENTS

WISHES FOR BABY

Guests

NAME & RELATIONSHIP TO THE PARENTS

_____

_____

MESSAGE OR ADVICE FOR THE PARENTS

_____

_____

_____

WISHES FOR BABY

_____

_____

_____

Guests

NAME & RELATIONSHIP TO THE PARENTS

_____

_____

MESSAGE OR ADVICE FOR THE PARENTS

_____

_____

_____

WISHES FOR BABY

_____

_____

_____

Guests

NAME & RELATIONSHIP TO THE PARENTS

_____

_____

MESSAGE OR ADVICE FOR THE PARENTS

_____

_____

_____

_____

WISHES FOR BABY

_____

_____

_____

Guests

NAME & RELATIONSHIP TO THE PARENTS

_____

_____

MESSAGE OR ADVICE FOR THE PARENTS

_____

_____

_____

_____

WISHES FOR BABY

_____

_____

_____

Guests

NAME & RELATIONSHIP TO THE PARENTS

_____

_____

MESSAGE OR ADVICE FOR THE PARENTS

_____

_____

_____

_____

WISHES FOR BABY

_____

_____

_____

Guests

NAME & RELATIONSHIP TO THE PARENTS

_____

_____

MESSAGE OR ADVICE FOR THE PARENTS

_____

_____

_____

_____

WISHES FOR BABY

_____

_____

_____

Guests

NAME & RELATIONSHIP TO THE PARENTS

_____

_____

MESSAGE OR ADVICE FOR THE PARENTS

_____

_____

_____

WISHES FOR BABY

_____

_____

_____

Guests

NAME & RELATIONSHIP TO THE PARENTS

_____

_____

MESSAGE OR ADVICE FOR THE PARENTS

_____

_____

_____

_____

WISHES FOR BABY

_____

_____

_____

Guests

NAME & RELATIONSHIP TO THE PARENTS

_____

_____

MESSAGE OR ADVICE FOR THE PARENTS

_____

_____

_____

WISHES FOR BABY

_____

_____

_____

Guests

NAME & RELATIONSHIP TO THE PARENTS

_____

_____

MESSAGE OR ADVICE FOR THE PARENTS

_____

_____

_____

_____

WISHES FOR BABY

_____

_____

_____

Guests

NAME & RELATIONSHIP TO THE PARENTS

_____

_____

MESSAGE OR ADVICE FOR THE PARENTS

_____

_____

_____

WISHES FOR BABY

_____

_____

Guests

NAME & RELATIONSHIP TO THE PARENTS

_____

_____

MESSAGE OR ADVICE FOR THE PARENTS

_____

_____

_____

WISHES FOR BABY

_____

_____

_____

Guests

NAME & RELATIONSHIP TO THE PARENTS

_____

_____

MESSAGE OR ADVICE FOR THE PARENTS

_____

_____

_____

WISHES FOR BABY

_____

_____

_____

Guests

NAME & RELATIONSHIP TO THE PARENTS

_____

_____

MESSAGE OR ADVICE FOR THE PARENTS

_____

_____

_____

_____

WISHES FOR BABY

_____

_____

_____

Guests

NAME & RELATIONSHIP TO THE PARENTS

_____

_____

MESSAGE OR ADVICE FOR THE PARENTS

_____

_____

_____

_____

WISHES FOR BABY

_____

_____

_____

Guests

NAME & RELATIONSHIP TO THE PARENTS

_____

_____

MESSAGE OR ADVICE FOR THE PARENTS

_____

_____

_____

_____

WISHES FOR BABY

_____

_____

_____

Guests

NAME & RELATIONSHIP TO THE PARENTS

_____

_____

MESSAGE OR ADVICE FOR THE PARENTS

_____

_____

_____

_____

WISHES FOR BABY

_____

_____

_____

Guests

NAME & RELATIONSHIP TO THE PARENTS

_____

_____

MESSAGE OR ADVICE FOR THE PARENTS

_____

_____

_____

_____

WISHES FOR BABY

_____

_____

_____

Guests

NAME & RELATIONSHIP TO THE PARENTS

_____

_____

MESSAGE OR ADVICE FOR THE PARENTS

_____

_____

_____

_____

WISHES FOR BABY

_____

_____

_____

Guests

NAME & RELATIONSHIP TO THE PARENTS

_____

_____

MESSAGE OR ADVICE FOR THE PARENTS

_____

_____

_____

WISHES FOR BABY

_____

_____

_____

• GIFT RECEIVED • • GIVEN BY • THANK YOU NOTE SENT

GIFT LOG

• GIFT RECEIVED •	• GIVEN BY •	THANK YOU NOTE SENT
		○
		○
		○
		○
		○
		○
		○
		○
		○
		○
		○
		○

• GIFT RECEIVED •   • GIVEN BY •   THANK YOU NOTE SENT

• GIFT RECEIVED •   • GIVEN BY •   THANK YOU
NOTE SENT

• GIFT RECEIVED •   • GIVEN BY •   THANK YOU
NOTE SENT

• GIFT RECEIVED •   • GIVEN BY •   THANK YOU NOTE SENT

• GIFT RECEIVED •   • GIVEN BY •   THANK YOU
                                       NOTE SENT

• GIFT RECEIVED •	• GIVEN BY •	THANK YOU NOTE SENT
_____	_____	○
_____	_____	○
_____	_____	○
_____	_____	○
_____	_____	○
_____	_____	○
_____	_____	○
_____	_____	○
_____	_____	○
_____	_____	○
_____	_____	○
_____	_____	○
_____	_____	○

Made in the USA
Columbia, SC
31 March 2025